Williams Sundial Properties:
Personal Computer Handbook!

Learn the basic operations
of your Personal Computer:
Then you can buy and install your own
without the need to hire a Consulting Firm
to assist you with the Installation.

Author: Lonnie L. Williams

Xulon
PRESS

Dedicated to:

The Hundreds of Technicians who worked with me
at Northern Telecom; Booker Rentals;
and Williams Electronics.

Table of Content

Introduction

This Williams Sundial Properties: Personal Computer Handbook became necessary because it is so difficult to find all the information you need to understand how a Personal Computer work and how to purchase, Install and understand it in one place.

After Spending more than Thirty-Eight Years as a Trained Electronic Technician, I have an Associates of Science degree from Atlanta Technical College, in Electronics, An Associates of science in Mathematics from Atlanta Metropolitan College, and I completed my 3rd year of Electrical Engineering at Georgia Institute of Technology (Ga. Tech.). I have a history with the purchasing, upgrading, and repairing of personal computers, and they make your life easier when they are working fine and they can become expensive door stops when they crash.

The more you learn about the operation of your own personal computer and how to install Software and Hardware and Upgrade the Software and Hardware Systems on your own, the more money you will save. Personal Computers can become very expensive if every time the computer freezes up, crash, or fail to come on, you must call an Electronic Technician, or Computer Tech. to restore it to operation.

I recommend that you read this book, the Williams Sundial Properties: Personal Computer Handbook was designed to give you the tools in one location to enable you

Williams Sundial Properties: A Computer Handbook!

to understand your Personal Computer well enough to enjoy it and not see it as a drain on you finances.

If you keep this Williams Sundial Properties: Personal Computer Handbook beside your computer and check it when you have a problem with your personal computer, you will find that you can do more things than you think you can when your computer fail. Also, you will see that the financial savings start to add up for you.

The History of Bus Slot Architecture for Personal Computers (PC)!

One of the most important features that you must consider when purchasing a Personal Computer (PC) is the Architecture that the Original Equipment Manufacturer (OEM) uses. This feature is very important in determining the true speed of the Personal Computer System. The main types of Input, Output (I/O) Buses or Architecture are:

(1) ISA Bus (Industry Standard Architecture Bus).
(2) EISA Bus (Extended Industry Standard Architecture Bus).
(3) MCA Bus (Micro Channel Architecture Bus).
(4) PCMCIA Bus (Personal Computer Memory Card International Association Bus).
(5) LC Bus (Local Bus)
(6) VL Bus (Video Local or VESA Local Bus, VESA (Video Electronic Standards Association)).
(7) PCI Bus (Peripheral Component Interconnect Bus).

The important feature to understand is that the main differences in these buses are the amount of data that they can transfer at one time and the speed in which they can do it. This is controlled by the Microprocessor that is connected to the main processing bus and the memory bus. If the Original Equipment Manufacturer uses a slow speed bus system only, then your Personal Computer's overall speed will be slow. Let us discuss each bus type further.

Industry Standard Architecture, ISA, is the type of bus architecture first introduced by **IBM** on the original IBM Personal Computer, (PC). The IBM PC was first introduced in 1982. IBM later expanded the ISA bus technology on the IBM AT /PC. The ISA bus was reliable and allowed many Manufacturers to build systems with components that were interchangeable. The ISA bus is used in some PCs even today because of its reliability. The ISA bus was used with 8-bit and 16-bit processors bus and hard drive data exchanges.

Extended Industry Standard Architecture, EISA, in 1988 many leading manufactures and Vendors combined to develop a new standard to avoid paying royalties to IBM to continue to use the ISA bus technology. New PCs using EISA technology started to be marketed in 1989. The EISA system slots would support ISA adapter cards and had many of the features of the MCA card from IBM. Both the EISA and MCA bus systems provided 32-bit slots for use with 386 or higher microprocessor Systems. This was a significantly faster speed for data processing and hard-drive exchanges when a hard drive controller was used. The EISA bus mastering system was used to speed up the system. A bus master is an adapter with a separate processor that can execute operations separately from the Central Processing Unit, CPU.

The Micro Channel
Architecture Bus (MCA):

When IBM introduced the **MCA** bus this was the beginning of the 32-bit personal computer motherboard slots, personal computer motherboard cards, and the 32-bit microprocessor. The MCA bus was designed to handle 32-bits of data at one time. This was the beginning of a whole new generation of Personal Computers, PCs, faster, more powerful, the 386 Microprocessor. This was the development that led to the design of the EISA bus that could also process 32-bits of data at one time.

There are three (3) types of MCA bus slots used by IBM PCs. The second (2) types used extensions to the original MCA bus slots called Memory-Matched extensions to handle enhanced memory cards.

The third (3) types were called MCA Video Extension and contained a special video-extension connector.

Local Bus: When the technology of computer user began to gravitate toward more Graphics, the video portion of the information transfer began to lag or suffer. The Engineers began to research a way to access the faster processor bus that allowed direct access to the Central Processing Unit (CPU). This was the beginning of the Local Bus which allowed external devices to be tied directly into the Processor Bus which led directly to the Central Processing Unit (CPU). The first Local-Bus was developed by **Dell Computers** and **Intel** in a joint Venture in 1992. One of the main features of this technology to separate it from the older, slower technology was to make the slots different to ensure only the external devices that you wanted to access the high speed Processor bus would be allowed into these slots.

VESA Local Bus, (VL): **The VESA Local Bus** (Video Electronics Standards Association) also known as Video Local Bus because the main emphasis at the time was to find a way to speed up the processing of Video Graphics that was becoming so demanding, in order to take Personal Computers to the next Generation. As the 486 Technology arrived there was a need to increase speed. The VL-Bus technology could move 32-bits of data at one time between the Central Processing Unit and Hard Drive of Same Technology Video Systems at the full 32-bit Bandwidth. The VL-Bus had a full Bandwidth of up to 132M per second.

Peripheral Component Interconnect Bus (PCI): In June 1992 the PCI Bus was introduced. The PCI bus was updated in April 1993. This technology inserted a bridge Bus between the previously standard bus and the Central Processing Unit, CPU. This removed the need to tap into the processor bus for external devices. However, it required a completely new set of Processor chips called controller chips to extend the Processor Bus length. This design allowed the broad 132M per second data transfer or bandwidth. This design revolutionized the Personal Computer Industry.

The Personal Computer Memory Card International Association Bus (PCMCIA): this was a credit card sized expansion board made to fit into a small slot in smaller Computers. This includes Laptops, Notebooks and Palm sized computers. This design gave these small computers the expandability found in the larger personal computers. This technology created the standard that allows compatibility for all small computers.

The History of
Input/Output (I/O) Cards.

When dealing with Input/Output Personal Computer (PC) Data/Information Cards, you must learn to access and manage System Resources. These resources include:

(1) Memory
(2) Direct Memory Access Channels (DMA Channels)
(3) Input/Output Port Addresses (I/O Ports)
(4) Interrupt Request Channels (IRQ)

Memory: You must realize that all Adapters, I/O Cards/ devices ETC. uses memory. The type of memory used depends on the device. For example, your video card use hidden memory in what is called video buffers, some cards require memory in what is called ROM or Read Only Memory portion of your system. If you display a large volume of graphics, a portion of the system's memory is used to store this graphics during the time it is waiting to be displayed. The total amount of memory must be greater than the programs to be displayed.

Direct Memory Access Channels: A parallel or a serial port do not use A DMA channel However, a device such as a tape backup system often does. Devices that are not used at the same time may share a DMA channel. It is important to keep in mind that any devices that will be used simultaneously must have separate channels.

Interrupt Request Channels, (IRQs): A hardware interrupt is a signal sent to the Motherboard requesting that a hardware device be given priority or allowed to break in to perform a function. When an interrupt request is received by the motherboard, all data in the CPU register is saved in a stack, and then the memory addresses are checked to complete the request.

Input/Output Port Addresses, (I/O Port): Everyone want to attach devices to their PC to enjoy additional Capability, The I/O port addresses allow you to add a large number of external devices such as Scanners, Faxes, Printers and etc.. The two serial ports on your PC are configured as COM1 and COM2. The parallel port is configured as LPT1. You must use the I/O addresses to communicate with the I/O ports.

Starting in 1994 a new Technology called "Plug-and-Play Systems started to appear on the market. Specifications existed at that time for PCMCIA, ISA, MCA, PCI, SCSI, IDE CD-ROM Systems. The technology allowing "Plug-and-Play" is advanced enough to detect new devices that are added to you PC system. The technology automatically

Assign the I/O port addresses and etc., this prevent the IRQ conflicts addressed above.

Plug and Play BIOS > A specially designed BIOS for configuring Plug and Play devices, system boards and cards during and after the system power-up process. This is done using a BIOS enumerator.

BIOS enumerator: has the ability to recognize all the hardware devices on the motherboard of a Personal Computer, PC, using the Plug and Play Technology.

What to expect when purchasing a New Personal Computer!

A fully capable computer for home use and college students can be purchased for under $1000.00. I found a Personal Computer in the morning newspaper on **September 29, 2004**, with the following features for 999.95.

Example 1X Processor, 2.8GHZ
With DVD+/-RW Burner
512MB PC3200 DDR Memory
160GB 7200 RPM Hard Drive
DVD+R/+RW/-R/-RW/CD-RW Burner Drive
CD-ROM Drive
XXX Integrated 64MB Shared Video Graphics
I. Link/FireWire (EEE1394) Ports
USB 2.0 Ports
High Speed 10/100 Networking
56K, V.90 Fax Modem
Movie, Music and Photo Software included
Click to DVD" Software Included
Windows XP Home Edition

WSP RS610 #4054392 WSP

If you are a fan of YYY Processors and can live with less speed and less memory in a home use Personal Computer, this model was available for less than $600.00.

Example 11Y Processor PC with CD-RW Burner Drive and Windows XP Home Edition
128MB Memory
40GB Hard Drive
CD-RW Drive
Motherboard Integrated Graphics
High Speed 10/100 Networking
56K Modem
USB Ports
Windows XP Home Edition

WSP 6064 #3868607 WSP

Memory for Personal Computers, PCs
How Computer Performance Work!

One of the more complicated components of purchasing a Personal Computer (PC) is the process of understanding Memory. Most PCs allow you to increase the amount of memory that a PC have by adding Memory Modules called SIMMs (Single Inline Memory Modules). There is a vast difference between the total Memory of a Personal Computer System and the amount of the Total Memory available as Usable Memory. The portion of the Total Memory that is not available for your use is used by the PC system for a variety of purposes, such as, storage of Video Graphics information waiting to be displayed known as Random Access Memory (RAM), Read Only Memory (ROM), Upper Memory Area (UMA), High Memory Area (HMA) and etc.. Therefore, when you see the Total Memory that a PC has, it is always a good idea to investigate further to determine the amount of Usable Memory that the Personal Computer System have.

I am listing some important Memory Terms and their Definition:

Random Access Memory (RAM) RAM is a form of Memory used as a temporary storage in PCs as needed when the pc is in use. The data stored is lost when the power is removed. The first 128K of Memory after Conventional

Memory defines video RAM. RAM is temporarily stored on chips that your computer uses to run the Operating System, like Windows, and other programs. The more RAM your computer has the faster your program will generally run.

Virtual Memory _ This is memory used by the operating system, like Windows, if your system lacks the random access memory (RAM) needed to run a program or operation. Virtual memory uses extra hard drive space in combination with the available computer's (RAM) to run programs. When Ram runs low, virtual memory moves data from RAM to a space called a paging file. The process of moving data to and from the paging file frees up RAM to complete its normal duties.

Read Only Memory (ROM) ROM Memory is a predefined prominent Memory that holds a specific data content. This Memory is not lost when the power is removed. Read Only Memory is Built-in Computer Memory that can be read by a computer but normally will not be changed by the computer owner.

Upper Memory Area (UMA) UMA Memory is the top 384K of reserved Memory in the first Megabyte of system Memory.

Single In-Line Memory Modules (SIMMs) SIMMs are single plug-in Memory Modules that are available in 30-pin, 9 bits or 72-pin, 36 bits combinations that can be used to add Memory capacity beyond that of the main Memory Chips.

Once you understand the concept of the different types of Memory and the difference in the Total Memory and Total Usable Memory, you can begin to see why the Usable Memory help determine the speed and efficiency of the Personal Computer (PC) that you buy.

How Computer Maintenance Work!

(1) What is a Fire Wall?

Firewall - This is Computer Software or Hardware written or designed to check all information coming from the Internet or other Networks, and based on your desired settings, will block or allow the information to pass through to your Computer.

Hard disk - The Primary Storage Device located inside the computer and sometimes referred to as the hard drive, hard disk drive, however referenced it is where the files and programs are permanently stored in your computer.

Virus - A Program that continues to reproduce itself. It spread by making copies of itself on a computer or by adding or inserting computer code into program or operating system files. Most Viruses damage files, some do not, some Viruses damage your computer, others do not, and however, they always affect a computer performance and stability because they use Memory and Hard Disk space. In order for a Virus to affect a computer or to spread, you are required to turn it on some how, such as, open an infected e-mail attachment or click on an unsolicited e-mail, document or file.

Restore Point - There is a built in program in your computer called System Restore. It can restore your system at specific intervals and when it detects the beginnings of a change to your computer.

Safe Mode - When you start your computer in the Safe Mode it gives your computer limited access to the operating system such as, Windows, and allows **Troubleshooting options.**

(2) What is a Strong Password?

Strong Password - A strong password is a password that cannot be easily cracked, guessed, or hacked. In a strong Password you will include LETTERS, NUMBERS AND UPPER CASE CARACTERS such as (!@#$%^&*).

(3) What is System Recovery?

System Recovery - The Process of restoring a computer hard disk with a damaged, corrupt, blank, or unresponsive hard disk drive to the state it was when it was manufactured, tested and programmed.

System Recovery Disks - A set of disks with a copy of all the files stored on the hard drive burned to CDs or DVDs with an easy to use software program included on your computer.

System Restore - System Restore will allow your computer's system files to be restored to an earlier point in time. This allows you to undo system changes to your computer without changing your personal files like photo albums, and e-mail folders.

Disk Cleanup - A program that frees up space on your hard disk drive by removing temporary and unused files.

Disk De fragmentation - The process of consolidating fragmented files on your computer's hard disk. Over time, both the file and the hard disk itself become fragmented; this can slow down your computer because it has to look many places to open a file.

Driver - This is Software that enables hardware devices such as a printer, mouse, and keyboard to work with your computer. Every device you add to your computer need a driver for it to work with the computer.

Malicious Software - This is software designed to deliberately harm your computer. This includes Viruses, Worms, Trojan Horses and other Malicious Software.

Malware - another name for Malicious Software.

Steps to take to
Prevent Computer Crashes

Studies show that a high number of the computer crashes are caused by poor use of your computer system. Sometimes too many programs installed on a hard disk while other programs or processes are running in the background can cause conflicts.

Any time a software program can not get enough memory from the operating system to complete a task, the program or computer or both can freeze or stop operating altogether. However, if memory can be recovered, or the computer can assume access to memory and write over it, the program can continue.

To protect your documents, you should save your files often and always save before opening a brand new program.

To avoid computer freezes and crashes, it is recommended that you do the steps listed below:

(1) Update devices drivers and BIOS regularly.

(2) Always have an up to date Virus and Firewall Software Program on your Computer.

(3) Check and add (if necessary) System Memory.

(4) Turn off the Internet when not in use.

(5) feel free to run the Hardware Diagnostics Tool when needed

(6) Set only Necessary programs to open at Startup

(7) Run Disk Cleanup

(8) Run Disk Defragmenter

(9) Close Programs that you are not using

(10) Restart Your Computer System Several Times Daily.

(11) Close Documents not in Use.

(12) Keep System Information current.

How do I troubleshoot Performance Issues?

You may notice that your computer system performance is slowing down. This may cause concern as to how and why? Let us look at some reasons for these performance issues:

(1) Hard disk space is too low, this can appear as memory issues because you cannot run some programs you could run before because this prevent virtual memory, where hard disk space is used.

(2) Your Computer may have a Virus; viruses can take up Hard disk space and memory space through Replication.

(3) De fragment your hard disk drive, the computer has to go to so many places that the computer slows in performance.
   (A) Consolidate the files and folders stored on your computer system and improve your computer performance.

(4) Computer may have a memory problem, not enough random access memory (RAM)

(5) The Software drivers may be old or out of date and need to be updated or reinstalled.
   (A) A driver is software that allows your computer to communicate with hardware or other devices as

needed. If you do not install the correct driver software, the hardware or device you connect will not work properly.

(6) Your Computer System, Microprocessors speed may not be fast enough for the software that you are running.

What is Basic
Input/Output System (BIOS)

B asic Input/Output System (BIOS) - is a firmware Program built into Personal Computers that starts the operating system when you turn on your computer. This firmware Program is also referred to as system firmware. BIOS is part of the hardware of your computer and is separate from the operating system.

What can I do to maximize my Computer's Performance?

Here are some recommended Maintenance Schedules!

To do List	Daily	Weekly	Monthly	Quarterly
Run a Virus Check	X	X	X	X
Scan for Spy ware	X	X	X	X
Schedule Firewall check		X		
Check for Operating Sys. Update				X
Check for Driver Updates				X
Check, delete, File E-mails	X	X	X	X
Scan for Malicious Software		X	X	X
Scan for Aware		X	X	X
Back up Important Files		X	X	X
Optimize Performance			X	X
Optimize Your Internet Browser				X
Check, Update BIOS			X	X
Change your Passwords				X
Block Spam	X			
Check Security Settings			X	X

Microprocessors for
Personal Computers (Pcs)!

Computer: A data processor designed to perform unlimited computation, including arithmetic, logic operations, and etc., without a human touch during the process. It is a device capable of solving problems by accepting data, processing the information, and providing the results of the processed data. A computer comes in three distinct parts, (1) Input devices, (2) Central Processing Unit (CPU) and (3) Output Devices.

Computer Science: The Study of Computers and the Phenomena that occur when they are used that has become known as the Art and Science of Information and Data Processing.

Microprocessor: The Microprocessor determines how fast and how powerful the Personal Computer process the data introduced into the PC. The Microprocessors are the brain of the PC and is referred to as the Central Processing Unit or (CPU).

What are some of the areas that computers has caused Amazing growth in:

(1) Registrar for Major Colleges and Student Aids
(2) Librarian
(3) Internal Revenue Service Assistants
(4) Management Consultant
(5) Bank teller and credit assistants
(6) Highway and Transportation assistants
(7) Assist Law Enforcement as a weapon against crime
(8) Multitasking device for Engineering, Architects, Law Firms
(9) Medical diagnostician, Doctor Assistants, and Pharmacist assistants
(10) Sales Aids for Retailers
(11) Dating Service Assistants

You can clearly see that the computer has become the data processing unit of our times and continue to take on a more prominent role in our daily lives that make us more dependent on the computer.

Today every educated person must know or study the basic operations and applications of the personal computer. Today's student may not find a discipline more important as a preparation for work and earning a living in the twenty-first (21) century.

Computers have changed the way we conduct our Government, Industry, Schools and other business that govern our society, communities and neighborhoods.

Let's Look at Medical Advancements and its Value to Society!

President Barack Obama, stated during the selection of his Staff, that a great saving to the United States (US) Economy could be realized by converting the Medical Records of all the Medical files handled by the US Government into electronic files, that is, upgrading them from paper files to Electronic Files. The Electronic Medical Records was projected to be a cost saving for the American Tax Payers over time. This cost saving is yet to be realized, however, it shows how far the computer has come and how much we depend on it in our daily lives.

The computer will continue to grow in importance for Doctors, Nurses, and Hospitals in providing medical services. Where Computers are so valuable, and take the place of an extra employee sitting with each critical ill patient, is the area of (1) Monitoring Patient's Conditions, (2) Storing a Patients Medical Records, (3) Assisting the Doctor in the Diagnosis and (4) Centralizing Information Systems for all the Medical Professionals.

The other reasons that Computer Monitoring of the patient is so important is that it allows for the rapid retrieval and collection of readings so the Doctor can identify any dangerous conditions early enough to correct them before too much damage occur. The computer can then complete daily logs, charts and graphs of the patient's (1) Temperature, (2) Heart Rate, (3) Blood Pressure and etc.

Why is storing a Patient's Medical Records so important? When a patient is hospitalized, the doctor may complete twenty-five (25) to three-hundred (300) tests on him or her. Laboratories may complete billions of these tests per year. This increased numbers of tests are creating problems for a paper system to keep up. However, a computer can handle this data with ease and process it and provide an organized (1)System of Storage, (2)Logs, (3) Charts and (4) Graphs.

How can the Computer assist the Doctor with the Diagnosis? In today's hospitals you have computerized Magnetic Resonating Imaging (MRI) Diagnostic Equipment that assist the doctor in looking into the body at the Disease, and other thoroughly modern equipment that is available to the doctor to aid in Diagnosis.

The Computer also provides a Centralized Information System for all the Medical Professionals, by placing all common users on an Office or Hospital Computer Network setup for multiple users. Each Individual location only needs a Terminal, consisting of a Monitor, a keyboard and a cable tie in to the Network system through a File Server.

How to Set up Your Personal Computer and Get Started!

When you open the box the first thing you should look for is the Parts List and compares it to everything that you have in the box. Once you are sure that everything you purchased is there, it is time to assemble your computer.

(1) Inspect and set up the desk where you will be working with your computer.

(2) Place the Central Processing Unit (CPU) on the Desk or underneath or beside the desk or where you plan to locate it permanently.

(3) You need to have full access to the rear of the CPU during the assembly process and then it can be permanently stored next to, beside or at the back of the desk.

(4) Locate all the attachments that must be plugged into the Central Processing Unit (CPU). Look at the end of the cable that must be plugged into the CPU; each cable should be painted a different color, or color coded.

(5) If the Key Board cable is red on the plug in end, then, look on the back of the Central Processing Unit for a Red Female plug, to plug it in.

(6) This is the way you assemble all of you attachments to the CPU, You look at the color of the plug in end of the attachment, then you find the same color on the back of the CPU and plug it in until all attachments are attached.

(7) Now find the Power cord, which should have a female plug on the end, plug it on the A.C. Male plug on the back of the CPU and plug it into the nearest A.C. Wall Socket and turn the computer on. Most computers take from 30 seconds to 11/2 minutes to turn on fully.

(8) This is a good time to find the individual instruction book that came with the individual model computer that you purchased. The assembly Process is Complete.

(9) If for any reason your computer do not come on at this time:
   (A) Check the Wall socket that you plugged the A.C. Cord in to make sure it works.
   (B) Check all plugged in attachments that you plugged into the CPU to ensure that they are installed correctly. Also, verify colors and make sure the light blue mouse is not plugged into the dark blue speaker plug!
   (C Check to ensure all Items are turned on!

(10) If you install any software, make sure you read the registration number carefully during the registration process. Sometimes, a B look like an 8 and O look like 0 and ETC. I have heard of Technical Personnel spending hours on the installation of one Software Disc. That should take minutes.

How to get Help from Technical Support When Your Computer Fail to Operate Properly!

The techniques that I am going to list will work for your computer, Printer, Digital Camera, Video Game or other expensive High Technology Item. At some point, you will need to deal with Technical Support for that product. Here are some tips that can make it easier:

(1) You should always list out the problems that you need to discuss in advance, write out a description of your problem in as much detail as you can, that way when you talk to Technical Support you will be able to tell them what the problem is. If the failed unit list error codes, now is the time to make them known.

(2) Always have the Model Number of the Failed Item you plan to discuss with technical support, (such as Your Computer, Video Game, and Printer and ETC.) this number is always needed. If it is your computer you will also need the version of operation system you are using, such as windows, if your high speed internet service fail you will need the modem and version of internet explorer you are using.

(3) You should always be polite for several reasons, (A) You get more help when you are helpful and polite (profes-

sional) than when you are frustrated and rude, (B) The phone calls are recorded.

(4) It is a good idea to use a Cell Phone or a Cordless Phone to make the call because if the call is long you can move around and if they ask for information you do not have in front of you, you can continue the conversation while retrieving this new information.

(5) You must be Assertive when you talk to the Technical Support Personnel in order to get your problems solved. If you have talked to an associate for a considerable amount of time and the problem is not being solved, ask to speak to the Supervisor, you will find that many companies have their support in layers. The first layer answer routine questions, the next layer are the repair/technical area and the third layer is the Management/Supervisory Level. Ask for what you need!

(6) If more Information is needed from you, by the Technical Support Personnel, before the problem can be resolved, write down the name of the person that you are talking to, get an e-mail address if possible, a direct number to this person so you do not have to start from the beginning the next time you call.

(7) If no more information is needed from you but it will take a while for Technical Support Personnel to resolve the problem, by ordering parts, or referring it to a Technical Group in your area, or having a Technical Support Personnel call you back, make sure you write down the name of the person telling you this, get any other information that you can, an e-mail address, a direct number to them and to the department or personnel they are referring.

(8) While you have the Technical Support Personnel on the line get warranty details, find out if they will replace the item if they cannot repair it. If the person you are speaking with cannot help, ask to speak to their manager, continue to elevate the issue until you resolve it. Always remember to be Assertive not Aggressive.

Universal Plug and Play Technology!

Universal Plug and Play (UPnP) Technology is a set of Networking Protocols Established by the Universal Plug and Play Forum. The goals of Universal Plug and Play are to allow devices to connect seamlessly and to simplify the implementation of networks in the home for data sharing, communications, and entertainment and in corporate environments for simplified installation of computers and their components. Universal Plug and Play achieves this by defining and publishing UPnP device control protocols (DCP) built upon open, Internet based communication standards.

The term Universal Plug and Play (UPnP) is derived from plug - and - play, a technology first introduced by Microsoft Corporation with windows, found a smarter way of attaching devices directly to a computer, however, UPnP is not directly related to the earlier PnP Technology. UPnP devices are PnP in that when connected to a network they make their presence known by presenting their network address automatically along with supported devices and service types, enabling clients that recognizes those types to begin using the device immediately.

UPnP is a distributed open architecture protocol based on established standards such as TCP/IP, UDP, HTTP, XML, and SOAP. The UPnP technology allows peer-to-peer networking of PC s, networked office/home appliances, CE devices and wireless devices.

The beauty of this is the fact that the UPnP architecture support zero-configuration networking. An UPnP compatible device from any Original Equipment Manufacturer Vendor can join a network, obtain an IP address, announce its name, convey its capabilities upon request, and learn about the presence and capabilities of other devices. DHCP and DNS servers are optional and are only used if they are available on the network. Devices can enter and leave the network automatically.

In December, 2008, The UPnP was published as a 73 part International Standard, ISO/IEC 29341.

UPnP technology can run on many media that support IP including Ethernet, Fire wire, IR (IrDA), home wiring, (G.hn) and RF (Bluetooth, Wi-Fi). No special device driver support is necessary; common protocol is used instead.

Any Operating System and any Programming Language can be used to build UPnP products. OS vendors may create APIs that suit their customer's needs.

UPnP architecture also enables conventional applications programmatic control.

Each UPnP product can have device-specific services layered on top of the basic architecture.

The next step in UPnP networking is event notification, this is sometimes referred to as "eventing". The event notification protocol defined in the Universal Plug and Play (UPnP) Device Architecture is known as GENA, this is an acronym for General Event Notification Architecture (GENA).

There is one serious concern with UPnP, and this concern the Lack of Default Authentication, The device you purchase to use must be able to perform their own authentication mechanism or they can leave your Firewall Vulnerable. A malicious website can manipulate your Router or Firewall using Silent Code.

How to Install Software on Your Computer!

(1) Insert CD/DVD into your CD/DVD drive if the software installer does not open automatically, double click the disk icon on your desktop, and in the resulting window, and look for a file with the word installer in the title or a package (.pkg) file. Double click the file to open the installer and follow the onscreen instruction to install the software. You can also use the Internet to download software.

(2) If you are using a downloaded file to install or update software, if you do not see an installer file, you can double click the down loaded disk image file to mount the disk image on your desk top. Double click the disk volume and then double click the installer or updater file. If no installer file appears, you can install the program by dragging and dropping the software from the disk image to the Applications folder or other folder on your Macintosh Computer.

How to Install Windows XP/Windows 7 on Your Computer!

The most popular Operating System used by personal computer makers, Original Equipment Manufacturer (OEMs) is Windows, and its most current version is Windows 7. The Operating System will allow your PC to run other Software, such as Games and Word Processors, spread sheets and graphics software. The Operating System must be able to interface between the Software you install and the Hardware of the Computer. The interface with the Hardware is through the Firmware, discussed earlier, called BIOS, or the Basic Input/Output System. The Operating System, Windows, connects the Software to the Hardware (to the hardware Via the BIOS) by acting as the interface between the two and allowing them to talk (communicate) with each other.

Without the BIOS Firmware your computer would never start up when you turn it on. Your computer's BIOS specify the search order that your computer uses to find a bootable operating system. The BIOS also determine the order in which the computer's attachments are checked to see if they are o.k., for example, it will check the (A) Floppy Drive first, then, (B)the CD/DVD drive, then, © the Hard disk drive, (D) any other removable disk in order of attachment, along with the printer and etc.. If the BIOS do not find a bootable operating system that includes an operating system, a failure code will be issued.

(1) To install the Operating System, simply place the CD/ DVD in the CD/DVD drive and reboot/restart the computer and when the BIOS check the CD/DVD drive it will start the CD/DVD, or give you a set of instructions on the desktop/screen to follow. If there are multiple disks, when the first is installed, the BIOS firmware will request the second disk until the process is complete.

(2) When installing the Operating System, Windows, it does not matter if it's from Microsoft or one of the Computer Manufacturers, Original Equipment Manufacturer (OEM) it should be a simple function. When you place the CD/DVD in the drive, you should immediately be taken through a series of screens, including a welcome screen, You are now set to Install, Press the "Enter" key or "Next" key, whichever is indicated on the screen.

How to Install and Troubleshoot the Hardware on Your Computer!

(1) Make sure the A.C. Cord is Unplugged and your com puter is turned off!

(2) Open the Desktop or Tower cover, using the proper tools, and remove the top cover.

(3) Remove and insert the hardware correctly in the mother-board slots. Make sure the new units are seated properly in the sockets making good contact or you may have an intermitted failure. If you are adding memory, normally there are extra slots for adding RAM memory. Again, remember to press firmly to ensure good connection.

(4) Close the case by reversing the process used to open it. Reconnect and restart computer.

(5) Insert the Installation disk into the disk drive once Windows load.

(6) Follow the Instructions provided by the installation disc., check to see if a driver was included with the material sent.

(7) There are exceptions to turning of your computer to add hardware, this include PLUG and PLAY Hardware. You just plug these devices with this Technology into your

computer and Windows will automatically detect the hardware and enable it.

(8) You should always read the manufacturer instruction to ensure that you are following the proper procedures when you plug this hardware in.

(9) Insert the hardware's included setup CD/DVD. On the CD/DVD you will find the drivers necessary to make your hardware operate as designed.

(10) Always contact the Technical Support Personnel when a serious problem occurs. Only try to fix the serious problems if you are technically trained to avoid electrical shock.

(11) Always choose new hardware that is compatible with the hardware that you are using, Multiple errors can occur with incompatible Hardware. Some computers are easier to repair by design than others. If you plan to upgrade your own, it may be a good idea to look at this before purchase.

(12) When looking for hardware it is a good idea to choose hardware that states on the box that it is Windows-Compatible, if you are using the Windows operating system. The Windows-Compatible label o0n the box means that it has already been tested for compatibility with Windows.

How to Protect Your Personal Computer with Firewall Software!

Firewall Software - A technology that helps prevent unwanted intrusion of unauthorized users from accessing your computer and its data via the Internet or other network, a firewall keep unauthorized data from entering or leaving your computer system.

Firewalls can block malicious attacks from mal ware, hackers and ad ware on your personal computer, and protect from outside threats. When a hacker target your computer, they want your tax return, password, bank checking, or bank saving account number, or even to hijack your computer for illegal purposes.

A Firewall can prevent an intruder from accessing your personal computer, either from the Internet or other network.

A Firewall will block some Trojan horse program and many malicious software applications that try to take over your computer.

A Firewall is most economical if purchased as part of a Suite. That mean, you purchase the Anti-Virus Software, Firewall Software, Anti-Spy ware Software, and

Anti Ad Ware Software in one package called a Suite. These Suites are tested together and are compatible and will not cause your computer to experience the conflicts that you will have if the firewall and Antivirus programs are from different vendors. When you connect to the Internet, you are sending and receiving data in small units called packets. A packet contains the addresses of the sender and the recipient along with a piece of data, a request or a command, or your connection to the Internet security information. This is the kind of information the Malicious Software is aiming for. A good Firewall carefully examines each data packet sent or received by your computer to see if it meets a set of criteria per your security setting. The Firewall then selectively passes or block the packet based on the results.

What criteria does your Firewall use to pass packets along? The criteria your Firewall uses to pass data along depend on the type of firewall that you are using. The most common type of firewall for small business and home use is called an Application Gateway Firewall. An application gateway, often called a proxy, acts like a customs officer for data: Anything you send or receive stops first at the firewall, which filters packets based on their IP addresses and content, also based on the specific functions of an application. An example, if you are running an FTP program, the proxy could permit the file to upload while blocking other FTP functions, this could include viewing and deleting files.

Another Firewall is: Packet Filters - which examines every packet for an approved IP address.

Another Firewall: Circuit Level Firewall - which allow communication only with approved computers and Internet service Providers.

Another Firewall type: Stateful Inspection Firewall - This Firewall check the configuration of approved packets and then pass or block traffic based on those characteristics.

During a serious compatibility test, the results showed that all Firewalls are not the same. Based on the results, I recommend two as having the fewest compatibility problems of the ten (10) tested.

(1) BlackICE Defender worked well with all the programs tested.

(2) McAfee.com finished close behind.

Norton and ZoneAlarm were the two with the next fewest compatibility issues.

Trojan Horse - A malicious program appearing to be a harmless piece of software that may be sent to you in an e-mail attachment or a download that you open and run. Trojan Horse programs are avenues for hackers to attack your personal computer.

Stealth Mode - A protection setting that hides a port so it is not seen over the Internet.

Port Scan/Port Probe - Data sent over the Internet by a hacker to locate your Personal Computer or Network and determine if it has open ports that will accept a connection.

Malicious Software – Software designed to deliberately harm your personal computer, for example, Viruses, worms, Trojan horses and etc..

IP (Internet Protocol) Address - The Identifying number of a Computer or other device. When two machines are connected directly to the Internet they cannot have the same IP address at the same time. Computers with static IP addresses (DSL or Cable modem connections) always use the same IP addresses; those with dynamic addresses (dial-up connections) are assigned a new IP address each time they log on to the Internet.

Hard Drive – The Primary storage device located inside your personal computer.

Hacker - Anyone who gain unauthorized access to others computers, without their knowledge or permission.

Fire Wall Software – This is software designed to check all information coming from the Internet or other Network, and based upon its security check, Blocks or pass the data through to your Computer.

Distributed Denial-of service (DDoS) Attack - using multiple computers to launch a DoS attack by gaining access to several outside computers and using them to launch the attack.

Denial-of Service DoS) Attack - Flooding an IP address with data, causing computers to crash or lose their connection to the Internet.

My fellow computer owners and purchasers, you can see that a little knowledge on how a computer operate and the ways you can address issues when a problem arises, can help your day run smoother and save you some hard earned money in the process. I bid you happy Computer moments! Thank You!

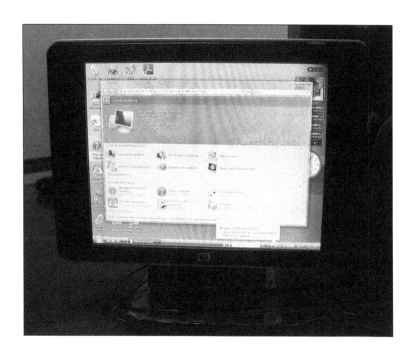

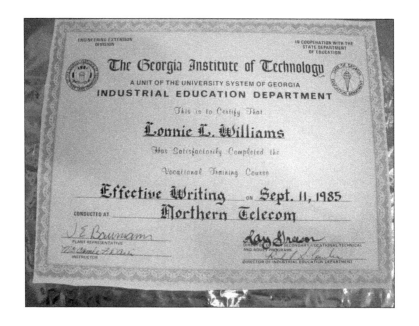

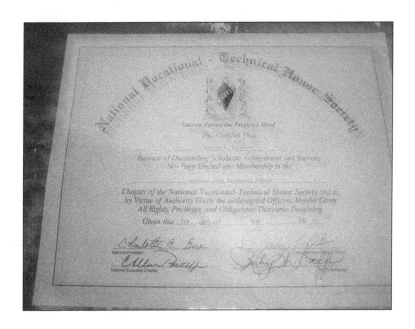

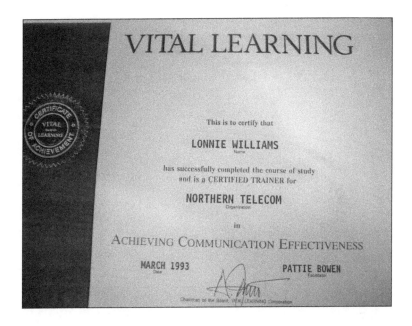

VITAL LEARNING

This is to certify that

LONNIE WILLIAMS
Name

has successfully completed the course of study
and is a CERTIFIED TRAINER for

NORTHERN TELECOM
Organization

in

ACHIEVING COMMUNICATION EFFECTIVENESS

MARCH 1993   PATTIE BOWEN
Date   Facilitator

Chairman of the Board, VITAL LEARNING Corporation

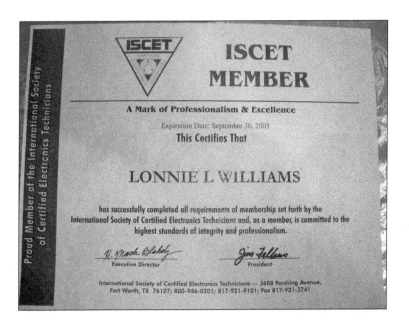

www.ingramcontent.com/pod-product-compliance
Lightning Source LLC
Chambersburg PA
CBHW051214050326
40689CB00008B/1307

* 9 7 8 1 6 0 9 5 7 1 0 2 3 *